Volume III

Bock's Best

All of the selections listed below are brand new arrangements and do not appear in any other Fred Bock piano book.

Publisher's note: This collection is the third in a series done by Mr. Bock. Volumes I and II of *Bock's Best* contain fifty arrangements each of hymns and gospel songs. If you enjoy playing the selections in this book, you will certainly enjoy the selections in Volume I (B-G0557) and Volume II (B-G0572). Available at your local music dealer (which is probably the same place you got this book).

FOREWORD

Button Up Your Overcoat—

As I sit here writing this Christmas piano book foreword (I've finally learned the difference between *foreword* and *forward*!) the weather outside is frightful: warm, about 92°, and the lyric content of *Jingle Bells* and *Away In A Manger* are simply not cooling me down! What I really should do is pour icewater over myself, and start dreaming of a white Christmas. I'm trying to get into a wintry, Christmas mood, but it's not easy, this business of writing piano arrangements out of season!

I think I've found the answer, though, and that's to sit myself down and play through all twenty-five Christmas piano selections in this new book. I have always wanted to do an all-Christmas collection. In some of my other piano books I've snuck in a Christmas piece or two just to round it out, but now to have one complete sourcebook of twenty-five—count 'em twenty-five—Christmas favorites everyone loves to play, is a dream fulfilled.

So, get yourself to a nice, in-tune piano, turn you calendar ahead to December, and play on. Here are a few of my favorite things: whiskers on kittens and my setting of THERE'S A SONG IN THE AIR. I must have been in a Chopin-esque mood that day, because this particular arrangement has many qualities of Chopin's piano etudes and nocturnes. Those chromatic lines need to be smoothly executed. "Practice makes perfect" (I didn't just make that up, but I'm 98% certain it's in the Bible somewhere), especially where there is a good deal of chromaticism involved. On the same day I wrote THERE'S A SONG IN THE AIR, I also wrote IT CAME UPON THE MIDNIGHT CLEAR. I'm not sure which came first (I really should discipline myself to using opus numbers) but I'm sure you'll catch the similarities. And then there's JINGLE BELLS. I debated with myself whether or not to include this song in the book, but then decided a definite "yes!" "Jingle all the way," says I. My thinking was that it simply is not possible to get through the holidays without someone, somewhere, wanting to *play* or *hear* this song. JINGLE BELLS is like Mom, Apple Pie, and the 4th of July, if you know what I mean. Now there are a few unusual notes and chords in this little number, so be careful little fingers what you play. I've made this list, and I've checked it twice, so *please* play the right notes on the chords in bars 3, 4, 5, 6, 7, and 8 of page 46. The notes are the same each time, only the octaves change. (See, I do try to make life easy for you piano players.) And, speaking of JINGLE BELLS, I did succumb to using the opening JINGLE BELLS motif a few times mingled amongst some of the other twenty-four carol arrangements. And just how many can you find? If you send me a letter clearly outlining page number, bar number, and score number where these excerpts can be found, and *if* you do find them *all,* I will send you a special gift. Send your cards and letters to me at Post Office Box 333, Tarzana, CA 91356-0333. This offer expires Christmas Eve.

If you are wanting to make some longer medleys out of these arrangements, feel free. Find the ones that fit together key-wise, and build a medley around a theme of your own. And don't forget about some of those other Fred Bock piano arrangements of Christmas tunes found in BOCK'S BEST #1 and #2.

With a happy Ho-Ho-Ho from sunny and warm Tarzana, California, I send forth these Christmas piano arrangements with lots of love. As you know, I actually *enjoy* writing piano arrangements, and from what I hear, many of you enjoy playing what I write. I hope this new book brings you happiness all year long, especially at Christmas, and even in June, September, or March.

Merry Christmas to all, and to all a good night.

Fred

FRED BOCK
Los Angeles, California

June, 1984

THE FIRST NOEL

ENGLISH MELODY
Arranged by Fred Bock

optional 8va
mp
mf
f
loco
8va
like chimes
8va

O LITTLE TOWN OF BETHLEHEM

LEWIS H. REDNER
Arranged by Fred Bock

accellerando
a tempo
mf
f
f
8va
8va
mf
f
8va
pp

IT CAME UPON THE MIDNIGHT CLEAR

RICHARD S. WILLIS
Arranged by Fred Bock

melody
strongly
ten.
15ma
15ma

SHEEP AND SHEPHERD MEDLEY

(WHILE BY THE SHEEP/WHILE SHEPHERDS WATCHED THEIR FLOCKS)

GERMAN MELODY
GEORGE F. HANDEL
Arranged by Fred Bock

firmly
mf
f
p
f
p
f
p
f
8va
ff
broaden
ff

GO, TELL IT ON THE MOUNTAINS

AMERICAN FOLK SONG
Arranged by Fred Bock

Brightly

even 8th notes
sub. mp

mp
mf
strongly
f

ten.
f
ff
ff
no ritard!
f
both hands 8va
slow
roll

LO, HOW A ROSE E'ER BLOOMING

GEISTLICHE KIRCHENGESANG
Arranged by Fred Bock

f
Ped.
mp
ten.
slowing
pp

GOD REST YE MERRY, GENTLEMEN

ENGLISH CAROL
Arranged by Fred Bock

8va
8va
8va
8va
f
mf
f
p
pp

AWAY IN A MANGER MEDLEY

1st tune - J. E. SPILMAN
2nd tune - JOHN R. MURRAY
Lullaby - JOHANNES BRAHMS
Arranged by Fred Bock

pp
melody p
mf
l.h.
slowly
rolled
pp

ANGELS WE HAVE HEARD ON HIGH

FRENCH CAROL
Arranged by Fred Bock

stronger
mf
simile

rit.
a tempo
f
pp
slowly rolled

SILENT NIGHT

FRANZ GRÜBER
Arranged by Fred Bock

8va
(b)
8va
8va
mf

strongly
l.h.
f
mp
mf
mp slower
mf
mp
pp

NOW IS BORN THE DIVINE CHRIST CHILD

FRENCH CAROL
Arranged by Fred Bock

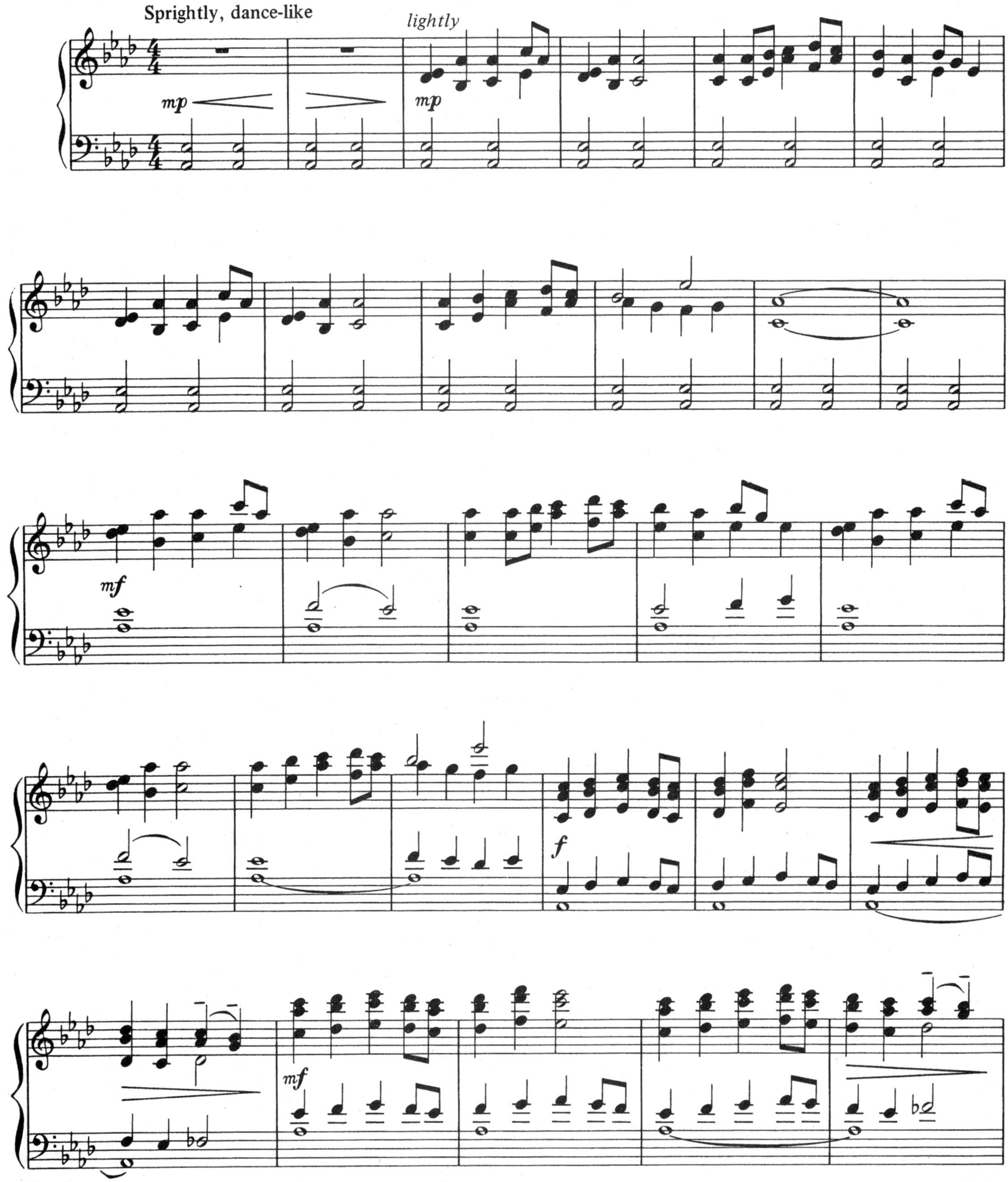

mp
f
strongly
f
mp
8va
8va

WE THREE KINGS

JOHN H. HOPKINS, JR.
Arranged by Fred Bock

pp
p
mp
mf
f
p
pp

THERE'S A SONG IN THE AIR

KARL P. HARRINGTON
Arranged by Fred Bock

f
mf
mp
p
mp
mp

GOOD KING WENCESLAS

TRADITIONAL CAROL
Arranged by Fred Bock

mp
mp
mf
a little more deliberate
f
mf
broaden
f
rit.
ten.
ten.
gradually resume tempo
brightly (like the beginning)
8va
f
ff
mf
r.h.
mp
8va
loco
mf
mp
8va
mf

JOY TO THE WORLD

GEORGE F. HANDEL
Arranged by Fred Bock

ff
ff
f
accented
smoothly
mf
8va
f
8va
8va
8va
8va
ff
8va
Ped.

DECK THE HALLS

OLD WELSH AIR
Arranged by Fred Bock

f
f
p
f
p
mf
8va
f
ff

WHAT CHILD IS THIS

ENGLISH MELODY
Arranged by Fred Bock

slowing
pp

O COME, O COME, EMMANUEL

PLAINSONG
Arranged by Fred Bock

strongly
tenderly
f
8va
8va
8va
8va
pp

JINGLE BELLS

J. PIERPONT
Arranged by Fred Bock

mp
f
mf
mp
p
l.h. over r.h.
mf
f
Ped.
Ped.

8va
15ma
8va
8va
15ma
8va
loco
loco
8ba
8ba
mp
mf

mf
f
mf
mp
8va
mf
mp
f

O HOLY NIGHT

ADOLPHE C. ADAM
Arranged by Fred Bock

ad lib.
slowing
broader 8va
8va
mf
mf
mp

WHILE SHEPHERDS WATCHED THEIR FLOCKS BY NIGHT

GEORGE F. HANDEL
Arranged by Fred Bock

f
f
slowing
ff
8ba

WE WISH YOU A MERRY CHRISTMAS

TRADITIONAL CAROL
Arranged by Fred Bock

f
8va
f 8va
loco
loco
ff
fff
8va

HARK! THE HERALD ANGELS SING

FELIX MENDELSSOHN
Arranged by Fred Bock

3
mf
f
3
ritard.
a tempo
8va
8va
ff

O CHRISTMAS TREE

TRADITIONAL GERMAN CAROL
Arranged by Fred Bock

8va
smoothly
mf
melody
8va
f
majestically
f
f
big and broad
8va

O COME, ALL YE FAITHFUL

JOHN F. WADE
Arranged by Fred Bock

f
slowing
f
8va
ff

. . . Merry Christmas to all, and to all a good night.